1. Interior of a shed at Steel Peech & Tozer, date unknown.

2. Bridgegate looking north in the late twenties. The White Hart is on the left. The business later moved across the road to a new building which afterwards became an office of the Halifax Building Society.

Memory Lane
Rotherham

by

John Tunney

3. Rotherham Bridge at a slightly later date than the photograph on the back cover. The chapel on the bridge was built around 1483 and Thomas Rotherham, Archbishop of York, is believed to have paid part of the cost. After the Reformation it became almshouses and between 1779 and 1826 a prison, which is why the name 'jail bridge' is sometimes used. The Bridge Inn was knocked down in the late twenties as part of the work for the new bridge, opened 1930. The new pub followed in 1933.

First published 1989 by
Archive Publications Ltd
Carrington Business Park
Urmston
Manchester M31 4DD
in association with
The Rotherham Star
18 Corporation Street
Rotherham S60 1NG
and
The Brian O'Malley Central Library & Arts Centre
Walker Place
Rotherham S65 1JH

Printed and bound in the United Kingdom by
Netherwood Dalton & Co Ltd, Huddersfield

ISBN: 0-948946-47-4

4. Lower Millgate about 1880. At 16 Bridgegate (*to the right*) George Dobson had a business as fruit, potato and provision merchant in 1876. By 1881 he had moved or gone out of business. Similarly Wards, the brush people, are mentioned in 1876 at 20 Bridgegate, but by 1881 Edward Russum had moved in.

Foreword

Photographs are one of the few sources we have that show what the past looked like and through the photographs in this book we can gain some idea of what it was like to live in Rotherham fifty or a hundred years ago. Many of the scenes depicted here have changed beyond all recognition. Many of the buildings illustrated have long been demolished, while a few still exist unchanged and others maintain a hidden existence behind modern facades.

This book has grown out of the (Memory Lane) supplement that appeared in *The Star* during February and March 1989. The supplement generated considerable local interest and a number of people contacted the Library to provide further information about some of the views that were featured. The photographs in the supplement and this book are drawn almost entirely from the thousands of photographs that comprise the illustrations collection of the Archives and Local Studies Section of the Brian O'Malley Central Library, Rotherham. The size and scope of the collection is due in no small part to the generosity of the many people who have donated photographs to the Archives and Local Studies Section or have loaned their treasured photographs for copying. In this book, it has been possible to use only a few photographs for areas outside the town of Rotherham. The collection, however, covers the whole of Rotherham Metropolitan Borough and includes views of the many other towns and villages that go to make up the Borough.

The staff of the Archives and Local Studies Section have enjoyed co-operating with John Tunney of *The Star* in the selection of the photographs and in the not inconsiderable research that lies behind the captions. The Library welcomes this opportunity to make at least part of the illustrations collection more widely known and at the same time cast light on the face of Rotherham in the past.

C C Williams
Director of Libraries, Museum and Arts.

5. The windmills in Doncaster Gate, once a landmark. They were built between 1774, when there is no sign of them on Rotherham's plan, and 1781, when they appear in a painting by Samuel Grimm. The 1851 map describes one of them as being 'old'. In 1873 they were owned by the trustees of E Badger, with an estimated rental of £8 and a rateable value of £16 6s. This picture was probably taken in the 1870s, shortly before they were demolished to make way for Percy Street.

Introduction

Spend just a few hours in the Archives and Local Studies section of Rotherham Central Library and you begin to realise something that might not be immediately obvious — there is an intense interest in the town's past.

The department is seldom, if ever, deserted. The microfilm machines whirr and click, pages rustle, and glass cabinets squeak open and shut.

There is a constant air of enquiry. It's not just family history they want; people are researching the history of buildings, plots of land, pubs. They want to know about coats of arms, who lived at number 32 in 1908 and when that pillar box was put in place. History in Rotherham is not a dusty, musty subject confined to the classroom — it is vibrant and alive.

Some of the recent visitors have been proving it. They wanted copies of pictures appearing in the *Rotherham Star's* Memory Lane series, which was intended to bring history to life. Sometimes the photograph simply captured the fancy; other times it showed people or buildings no longer with us.

In the case of the buildings there's a lot of choice. Few places can have changed as dramatically at the hands of well-meaning planners. In the case of slums, few could disagree with the demolition decision; in the case of ancient buildings and historic streets it might be a different matter. Some views of the old town make it look like Barchester or some other imaginary church-dominated town. The visitor would be hard pushed to find such a vista now.

But towns aren't primarily about buildings. They are about the people who built them, lived in them and laboured in them. That is one of the reasons why *Memory Lane Rotherham* has a lot of faces in it. They show the true character of the town.

The job of selecting and identifying the photographs would have been impossible without the Archives and Local Studies staff, who have cheerfully suffered weeks of disruption and cross--examination in the production of this book. In particular I must thank archivist Tony Munford for his meticulous correction and enlargement of captions; local studies librarian Freda Crowder for her vast knowledge and experience; assistant archivist Sally Shepard; Pat Hobson and Gill Lyon. Without their help the captions would have been very sparse. Queries to them are not a chore but a challenge.

We have made every effort to get things right; if mistakes have crept in, I apologise. Any additional information on the photographs in this book would be welcome.

Many thanks are also due to David Banks and Phil Dalton of *Sheffield Newspapers* for their skills in selection and presentation of the original Memory Lane material — as well as their encouragement.

John Tunney
April 1989

6. The boatyard on the Greasbrough canal, probably in the 1890s. The waterway was built by the Fitzwilliams a century beforehand to connect their coalmines to the Don Navigation at Parkgate. Fifty years later the top half was filled in, but the bottom bit remained in commercial use up to the First World War and the last boat used it in 1928. In the twenties one of the houses in the picture was the home of Jack and Daisy Staves, who brought up a family of seven in it. Six of them were born there. One of them, Mrs Joan Roper, was delivered at their two-up, two-down, home in 1923. There was no gas or electricity; rent was four shillings (20p) a week. "We were snided out with rats," she recalled.

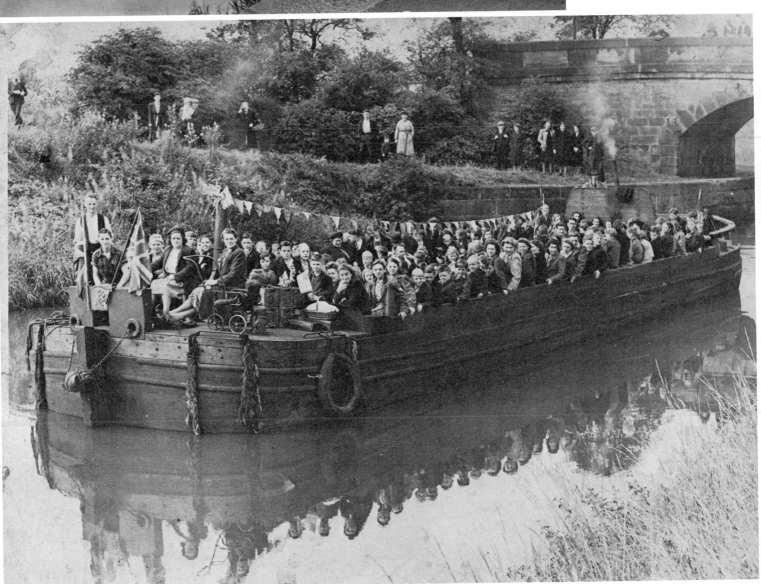

7. A water excursion at Aldwarke on VJ Day, 1945. The boat is the *Rowland,* built for canal carriers Waddington & Sons, of Swinton, and normally used for carrying coal to the glassworks on the canal. It had the distinction of being the first petrol-powered barge on the waterway, courtesy of a Buick car from which the engine had been removed.

8. *above:* College Street about 1890. The tobacconists known as the Old Number Twelve, demolished shortly before the picture was taken, stood out on the pavement on the right. The spot was later to become the entrance to Woolworth's.

9. *below:* College Street, almost certainly 1904. Trams were still a novelty; number 1 is on the Rawmarsh Road route and number 27 is in the background. The figure of the Scotsman above Stansfield's the tobacconists remained in place until redevelopment in the late twenties. He can still be seen in the Museum in Clifton Park.

10. *above:* College Street in 1926 or 1927. Fawley's the ironmongers are not listed in the directory for 1926, although their message to customers can clearly be seen in the picture. On the other hand, the buildings at the end of the street, beyond the Grand Clothing Company, were demolished by the time the 1927 directory was published. Jessie Horsfield the chemist was at number 1, boot dealers Levy Brothers at 1a and hosier J F Newton at number 3.

11. *below:* College Street, probably 1928. Hairdresser Thomas Cox operated in the street for around thirty years, first at number 6 and then at number 4. Boot and shoe dealer Catherine Walker had previously been at 6; Henry Hicks, the saddler, had earlier replaced Ellen Sharpe, who ran dining rooms and a confectionery business at 4. By 1929 Mr Cox had gone, presumably retired, and was replaced by druggist Frank Poyser.

12. *above:* The corner of High Street and College Street probably between 1881 and 1892. Scales and Salter, the boot and shoe people, are listed in business as early as 1872. Bookseller John Henry Boulton, who occupied number 1 High Street — the building on the left advertising the *Sheffield Daily Telegraph* — is first discovered there in 1881. The premises were demolished in 1892.

13. *below:* Ann Craig's shop at 12 The Crofts about 1881. Mrs Craig, described in that year as being a grocer aged sixty, may have been the widow of Andrew Craig, a shopkeeper in Wellgate in 1871. The first mention of Ann is in Thornhill, Masbrough, in 1872 and then in Drummond Street in 1876.

4. Doncaster Gate almost certainly in 1914.
The Cinema House on the left opened just before the war broke out. Scales's shop is in the
centre of the picture on the corner of High
Street, while the King's Arms and Wheatsheaf
are both on the right.

15. Imperial Buildings corner before the First
World War, prior to the development of Ship
Hill. The Cross Daggers is on the site that later
became part of the Empire Cinema. A boy plays
with a hoop, a girl pulls her stockings up and in
the background a tramways water cart goes
about its business. Tram number 31 was the
town's water trailer at that time — the vehicle
was needed to clear the tracks of debris.
Imperial Buildings, opened in 1908, replaced the
early nineteenth century Shambles and the shops
at the top of the High Street, allowing the
notorious bottleneck there to be widened.

. Guns in Clifton Park after World War One.
he two cannon were a gift to the town in 1905
om T W Ward of Sheffield, who had been
eaking up old men of war. The central gun
as given to the town by the government after
e war, in recognition of the efforts of towns-
ople for Britain. The council resolved to re-
ve them in 1937.

17. The view over the weir near Aldwarke Hall as it was towards the end of the nineteenth century. The eighteenth century big house, ancestral home of the Foljambe family, was demolished in 1899 by the colliery company which had bought it some years earlier. The building on the right is Aldwarke House, not to be confused with the hall. In the distance is Dalton Brook Mill.

18. The entrance to the hall about 1895.

19. The gates just before demolition as the Parkgate works were extended in 1961.

20. Clear air, hardly any smoke in sight, even from the gasworks. The reason is simple — the 1926 miners' strike, meaning little or no coal. This shot of the town's roofscape was taken from the parish church. Bridgegate is in the left foreground, while the chimney of Mappin's brewery can be seen extreme left.

21-22. *left:* Bridgegate with flags out, possibly either for the opening of Clifton Park in 1893 or Queen Victoria's Jubilee in 1897. *above:* The White Hart, from Millgate in the late twenties. The churchyard wall is on the right.

E.L.S. 172-110 Bridgegate, Rotherham.

23. *left:* Bridgegate in the early twenties. This picture is taken from a postcard sent on 23 December 1921. Russum's hardware store is at number 29. Edward Russum was the son of a Leeds brushmaker. He moved to number 20 Bridgegate in 1880 or 1881 to premises in which brushes had already been made for at least ten years. The move across the street came in the 1890s and the retail side of the firm closed in 1981. The business continued as a supplier of catering uniforms and knives.

24. *right:* Bridgegate in 1952.

25. *below:* Bridgegate before it was widened in the late 1920s. The ancient building with its massive timbers is the Turf Tavern, one of many historic buildings that felt the weight of the demolition man's hammer.

26. The Turf again, this time from College Street. Posters reveal that Lon Chaney is appearing at the Empire in *Tell It To The Marines*, a film made in 1926. The Royal (the name adopted by the Theatre Royal, Howard Street, when it was converted to a cinema in 1916) was showing something called *Cool Hand Saunders*. In 1930, when it was equipped for sound, it changed name again, to the Regent Cinema.

27. High Street in 1908.

28. Sandwich board men in High Street, possibly in the late twenties. Burton's 55-shilling (£2.75p) suits were made from Laird Scotch Tweed. The tailors moved to the High Street shop some time between 1913 and 1922.

29. High Street in the late twenties or early thirties. Mason's watch and clock makers is clearly seen.

30. *left:* Rotherham's first car registration plate. The 10hp Wolseley was registered on 12 December 1903, in the name of solicitor Joseph Hardy Pickford, of Leafy Bank, Moorgate. It later became part of the fleet of hire cars owned by Moorhouse & Company.

31. *above:* The distinctive registration became the symbol of the mayor in later years. Here is the mayoral Austin Princess in April 1955, being polished by chauffeur Jack Barlow. The ET mark lends itself to the making of a number of useful words. When the Rover car company began experimenting with a gas turbine vehicle in the early fifties they were allowed by the Rotherham Motor Taxation office to jump the queue so they could have the registration JET 1. This revolutionary, but impracticable, car reached 150 mph on a Belgian motorway, but never ran on British roads. It is now in the Road Transport Museum in Coventry.

32. An ET in trouble. This was a crash near the junction of Broom Lane and Broom Road on 1 November 1935. Other photographs reveal hardly another vehicle to be seen. A survey of traffic in the area eleven years earlier revealed 2000 vehicles using Broom Road every day . . . 200 push bikes, 250 motorcycles, 350 cars, 300 vans, 325 buses (all types), 225 lorries, 20 traction engines, 50 light horse vehicles, 40 heavy horse vehicles and 100 electric trams.

33. An ET of a different kind. The identity of the two girls is a mystery — as is the location. What is certain is that the bike was a Triumph registered in Rotherham in 1923.

34. Outing from the White Lion, College Road, Masbrough, a pub popularly known as *The Dog*. The picture was taken between 1924, when *The People's Butcher* Jack Telling moved into number 90 to replace Ernest Allsopp, and 1934, when Samuel Glenn took over. Included in the trip are Jack Wright, George Jevry, some of the Graves boys, Fryer Barler, Jim Brailsforth and Alf Webb, thought to have worked at Rotherham Forge.

35. A fishing trip from the Eastwood Inn, Doncaster Road. The chara is a 1910 Sheffield-built Durham Churchill, top speed 12mph.

A line-up of locos at Canklow, bably early sixties, led by Stanier 0 8F.

37. A Stanier Black Five, number 44744, at Masbrough station probably in the fifties. St John's church, the building in the background, was opened on 30 November 1864, and demolished a century later.

he last passenger train from Westgate ion on 4 October 1952. Mayor M Young es hands with the driver of 40409. tgate was the first station in the town, ed in 1838 as terminus of the Sheffield Rotherham Railway.

39. The last passengers climb aboard for the last departure — the 5.27 to Sheffield.

40. The choristers are from St John's, in procession some time in the fifties to join their comrades from other churches for the Whitsuntide walk from Station Field to Clifton Park. The Station Field, for many years the site of the Statute Fair, later became the site of police headquarters.

41. The town's firemen, proud possessors of what is probably the Shand Mason steam fire engine, based at the station at the junction of Drummond Street and Rawmarsh Road. Other firefighting equipment included three horses, a tower wagon and ambulance. When the first motorised engine arrived the steam machine was put up for sale.

42. This may be the brigade's first motor powered machine. The 60hp Dennis cost the corporation £973 in 1914. The four cylinder petrol engine gave it a top speed of 40mph and it could climb a hill of one-in-six fully loaded. It was christened by the mayoress with a bottle of water in Clifton Park on 19 February and named *Progress*. The second motor was bought in 1919 after a serious fire at Oakwood Hall when *Progress* was being repaired.

43. An inspection at Rawmarsh Road in the 1930s. Note the breeches and boots. The move to the new station from Frederick Street was made in 1885. Early fire fighting was done from Petticoat Alley, in the now demolished Shambles.

44. A group at Erskine Road fire station, date unknown. The new station was officially opened on 27 April 1939 — a masterpiece of timing for what was to follow in September. It provided a base for four motor pumps and up to eight ambulances — and also kennels for stray cats and dogs. Twenty-four cottages were built nearby to house the firemen.

45. *right:* A World War Two fire fighting team at Steel Peech & Tozer man a Coventry Climax trailer pump on the river bank at the Ickles.

46. The ambulance service, except for t[ ] war years, was part of the fire brigade. [ ] stayed that way until 1 April 1974. T[ ] vehicle on the right is a Daimler, in [ ] picture taken around 1930.

47-49. PC's Progress: the young bobby Richard Parkinson, who lived at 75 Carlisle Street, was appointed Probationer Constable on 5 March 1900. He was aged 21, stood 5ft 11in, had a fresh complexion, blue eyes and was born at Thorpe, near Boston, Lincolnshire. His previous job was as labourer at Altofts, Normanton. *centre:* Sergeant's stripes. *right:* Inspector's baton.

50. With the bigwigs as Chief Inspector about twenty years after joining, sitting second left. Others seated are *from left:* Inspector B Hewson, Chief Constable Edwin Weatherhogg (who held the post 1907-32), Detective Inspector C Smith and Joseph Downing, Inspector and Superintendent of the Fire Brigade. Standing are *left to right:* Inspectors J Proudlove, C Nelson, O Northropp and E Myers.

51. More police, this time 'clearing the streets' during the 1911 rail strike. The location is believed to be Favell's shop in Masbrough Street.

52. A carter with police escort in Brinsworth Street, Masbrough, during the same dispute. The week-long national strike was over union recognition. A battalion of Gordon Highlanders was dispatched to Sheffield from Colchester without any request from the local authorities and a company of them turned up in Rotherham. They weren't needed. The dispute, which crippled industry in the area, ended on 20 August with a victory for the strikers.

53. A Clarion Van in the town on 1 October 1904. The vans were mobile political missions closely connected with the Independent Labour Party. They became an institution as they travelled the north preaching the gospel of socialism. Caroline Martyn was an early vanner who died in 1896, aged twenty-nine.

54. King Edward VII died on 6 May 1910. A fortnight later a memorial service was held at the parish church to mark his passing after nine years on the throne. The procession of civic dignitaries is seen entering College Square, led by the Mayor, Councillor D Mullins.

55. July 1912, and a royal party poses informally in front of Wentworth Woodhouse. King George V and Queen Mary were guests of Earl Fitzwilliam as they visited pit villages in the region. The two girls sitting on the carpets at the front are Lady Joan Fitzwilliam (*left*) and Lady Maud Lilian Elfrida Mary Wentworth-Fitzwilliam, who was to become mother of the fourth Earl of Wharncliffe. Both girls are holding their own cameras, obviously waiting for the professionals to get out of the way. Included in the aristocratic gathering are the Earl of Harewood, Marchioness of Londonderry and the Archbishop of York, Cosmo Lang, who was later to step up a rung to the archdiocese of Canterbury and figure in the furore of the abdication twenty-four years on.

56. The King and Queen were having a look round Silverwood Colliery when it was decided she would have too far to walk. A 'carriage' was summoned, consisting of a trolley provided by the Midland Railway. The beautifully polished shoes of the men pushing it suggest the move was not entirely spontaneous. Her Majesty was wearing a navy blue poplin coat, with revers faced with rose pattern silk crepe. The hat was tuscan straw, trimmed with roses in pink, blue and mauve and wheat ears of chiffon. The giggling attendants are Lady Aberconway (*left*), and Lady Eva Dugdale. The charm of this scene was to be overshadowed by a grim tragedy taking place a few miles away at Cadeby Colliery. On the same day an explosion killed 88 men and boys. The royal itinerary was changed to take in Cadeby the next day. The Queen wept as she left.

57. A Royal visit during the Phoney War, in December 1940. The then Princess Royal, Victoria Alexandra Alice Mary, great aunt of Princess Anne, is greeted by Lady Lawson Tancred as she arrives to inspect the Auxiliary Territorial Service and WRVS in the town. Westgate station and Main Street post office can be seen in the background. Princess Mary, born 1897, was sister of George VI and wife of the Earl of Harewood. The black band on her arm was mourning for her great aunt Louise, who died in December 1939. Lady Tancred came from Boroughbridge. She was to lose her eldest son killed in action 1944.

58. Thirteen years after the Princess Royal came another Princess, this time the Queen's sister Margaret. She is pictured here inspecting a guard of honour of men from the York and Lancaster Regiment and the 467th HAA Regiment of Rotherham. The escort is Major J V Hawkins and behind are Brigadier G C Robins and Colonel Stephen Rhodes.

For nine-year-old Judith Howard it was a tense, rvous occasion. The St John Ambulance Brigade rsing cadet had the job of presenting the Princess with ouquet after she left the parish church by the north or.

60. Other cadets and young nurses formed an aisle as the royal visitor arrived at the west door. The date was 19 April 1953, just a few weeks before the Coronation. Interest in the monarchy was running high and thousands turned out for the Saturday occasion.

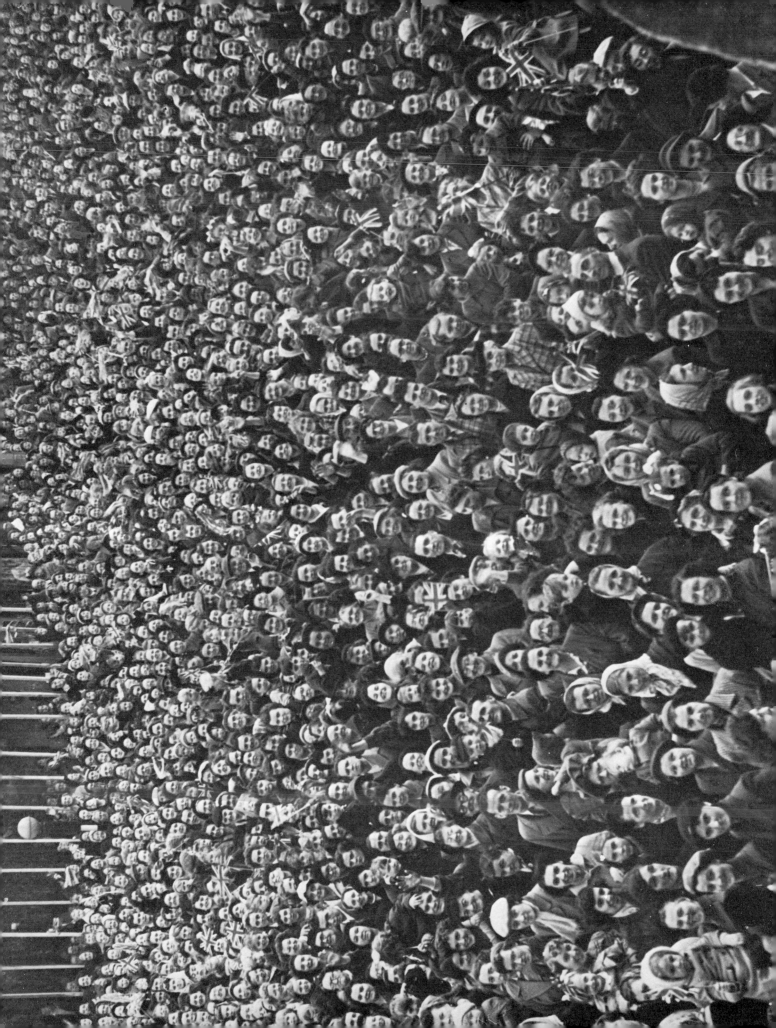

opposite page: Eighteen [mo]nths after Princess [M]argaret's visit it was the turn [of] her big sister. The young [Qu]een, accompanied by Prince [Ph]ilip, arrived on 27 October [19]54. A sea of faces waited [ea]gerly. This was the scene in [fro]nt of Brittain's furnishing [sho]p, looking up Howard Street [to]wards the Regent.

right: Crowds also gathered [at] other vantage points. This is [tho]ught to be the throng at the [cor]ner of the Bridge Inn.

below: The front of the [mu]nicipal buildings in [Fr]ederick Street was another [po]pular choice. It was a big day [no]t only for the town's bigwigs [as] they were introduced to the [mo]narch, but also for younger [pe]ople who met her as well. [Re]presenting the schools were: [Mi]chael E Rose, aged 18, Senior [Pr]efect at the Grammar School; [El]izabeth Mason, 17, Head Girl [of] the High School for Girls; [Ph]ilip Naylor, 16, School [Ca]ptain and Gwendolyn Smith, [He]ad Girl, both of Oakwood [Te]chnical High.

64. *opposite page:* Numbers 383 and 385 Doncaster Road at the time of the Coronation in 1953. The lady with the basket is outside Bayliss and Taylor's newsagents. Next door was the shop of William Wallace, while others in the block included Mrs Pearl Bird at 381 and draper John Dyson at 387.

65. *right:* Herbert Athey's shop at 451 Fitzwilliam Road the same year.

66. Doncaster Road again, also in Coronation year.

67. Corporation Street in 1935, looking south. Upper Millgate is in the left foreground. The property on the left was demolished to make way for All Saints Buildings, only half finished when war broke out. The photograph says the Hippodrome was showing George Brent and Bette Davis in *Special Agent*, while *Top Hat* and Fred Astaire were on at the Premiere.

68. The scene beside St Mary Magdalene's church at Whiston, about 1890. The buildings on the right became reading rooms in 1902.

69. A 'still life' taken on 16 September 1930. The School of Art in Frederick Street opened in 1888. A century later work began to transform it into a shopping centre.

70. Excitement is rife in Effingham Square. Time? Just before 1.30. Date? 20 June 1912. Occasion? Unveiling of the James Hastings clock tower.

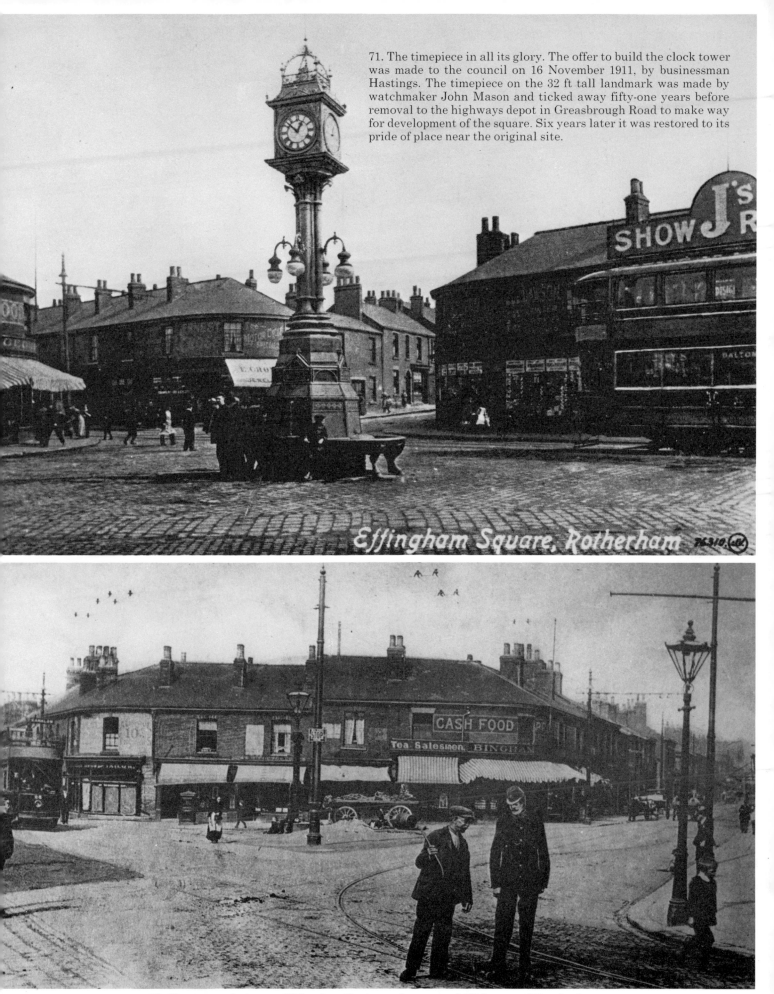

71. The timepiece in all its glory. The offer to build the clock tower was made to the council on 16 November 1911, by businessman Hastings. The timepiece on the 32 ft tall landmark was made by watchmaker John Mason and ticked away fifty-one years before removal to the highways depot in Greasbrough Road to make way for development of the square. Six years later it was restored to its pride of place near the original site.

Effingham Square, Rotherham

72. The square between 1903, when the trams began, and 1912, year of the clock.

73. Effingham Square in the late fifties.

74. The way we used to live ... dustbins and washing at the back of Shaftesbury Square, demolished in the 1960s.

75. Backyards may not have been pretty, but they were ideal gossiping places for young and old alike. This picture was taken in the Sheffield Road area, probably in the late fifties.

76. James William Parkinson takes a well-earned rest in a kitchen chair. He didn't have far to take it; the kitchen of 12 River Street probably opened directly on to the lane, off Sheffield Road. Mums didn't have far to take the washing, either. Not many people had cars in the fifties, so the chances of traffic disturbing the lines were not great.

The front of Shaftesbury Square, the first major housing development aimed at the working classes in Rotherham. It was built in 1855 by [Wil]liam Blackmore and rates a mention in Pevsner, the architectural bible, but that did not prevent its demolition. Standing on the right are [Mr]s Frances Egley, with daughters Wendy (*left*) and Doreen. Mrs Egley died in 1987. The picture was taken before the Coronation in 1953 because [the]ir father, a painter and decorator, placed a mural above the front door to mark the event. Wendy and Doreen said that the pram belonged to [Gra]ce Mackenzie, while the motorbike was Bill Moughton's from No 17.

78. Slum housing came under the scrutiny of the Medical Officer of Health and Borough Engineer's Department in 1933. The Westgate area was one that attracted particular attention. Oil Mill Fold as the Inspectors found it.

79. Further down the Fold, with advertisements for Keating's Powder (to get rid of fleas) and Wincarnis tonic wine (a genteel way to get rid of the blues). It was unlikely anyone living there could have afforded it. The street was named after a horse-powered mill that stood there in the eighteenth century.

80. Westgate Court. The kids are standing outside Walter Montgomery's hairdressers shop. Next door was shopkeeper William Douglas, then came butcher Alfred Telling and another shop run by John Wilkin. On the extreme left can be seen the gates of the parish church mission hall. Opposite used to be a pub called the True Briton. Pubs and beer houses were a feature of Westgate.

81. Lines of washing and a watchful woman in Oil Mill Fold. The directory of 1930-32 says nothing about it except that it was the location of H Handley's hardware dealers warehouse. Many of the houses had only a single room on each floor, but in 1933 they were home for up to seven adults and children . . . each. Weekly rents ranged from 4s 6d (22½p) to 6s 6d (32½p).

82. Downs Row, off Moorgate Street, 1933.

83. Behind the arches lies a story. This is Court 17, Masbrough Street, between Chapel Walk and Wentworth Street in 1935. The reason for the unusual appearance of the houses is that they were built as either coachhouses or other outbuildings of Masbrough Hall. In 1861 the row was known as Maltkiln Yard and an 1851 map shows a gate giving access to the grounds of the eighteenth century hall. It is possible the row was built in the same period. In 1881 thirty-seven people lived there. The Ebenezer Chapel was built on the site of the demolished hall and it later became a mosque; the Court 17 neighbourhood became part of the route of Centenary Way in the 1970s.

84. Boarded-up windows and drying combinations on 9 December 1935, belie the former grandeur of The Poplars, a house between Douglas Street and Quarry Hill. It was almost surrounded by a warren of courts in the nineteenth century. In the 1880s it achieved prominence as a 'hydropathic institute', a centre for Victorian water treatment. In 1898 the proprietor was Edwin Barnes and it closed in 1904.

85. Albert Street, between Station Road and College Road, in 1933.

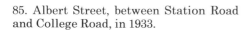

86. Thomas Street, another collection of terraced houses buried beneath Centenary Way. The Masbrough works can be seen in the background.

87. The rear of Thomas Street at the same time in 1933. The family potty is conveniently placed on the window sill.

88. Burrell Street, 1937.

89. The approach to the church steps from College Square in 1904. Pearsons the milliners are on the right and Smiths the drapers on the left. The mock half timbered building is the old Assembly Rooms, taken over by the White Hart as billiard rooms.

90. The steps in the 1890s. The Institute saw many uses: drill ha[ll], billiard rooms and chapel among them. H Blanchard, licensee at th[e] White Hart, moved around a bit. At different times he was landlord [of] the Red Lion, the Ship Hotel and Sportsman at Parkgate.

91. The rear of the White Hart in 1926.

92. A glimpse of what helped make Rotherham famous. The 600-ton plate blanking press in operation at the Park Gate Iron & Steel Company, probably some time in the 1930s.

93. A shot that marries the coal, iron and steel industry. Pit arches and props in production at Park Gate at the same date.

94. The demolition of the Park Gate blast furnaces in 1976. The first of them was completed in 1905 and they were the only 'modern' one to be built in South Yorkshire. The buildings on the left are the remains of the houses in Lloyd Street.

Fettling an open hearth furnace at Templeborough in 1949. The man on the right is the appropriately-named Eric Ironmonger. Fettling involves the repair of the lining of the furnace.

96. Harry Ellis, Templeborough open hearth melting shop furnaceman, preparing to take a sample in 1947. He is using a sampling spoon to knock in a wedge.

97. Sampling in the electric melting shop at Templeborough in the 1960s.

98. The nineteenth century work force of George Wright and Company gathered for a photograph. The man in the middle in the bowler hat could be George Wright, owner of the Burton Weir Stove Grate works at New York. The company moved to Rotherham from Sheffield in 1863 and the picture was probably taken twenty or so years later.

99. Phoenix Brass Band of Steel Peech & Tozer some time in the 1930s. The picture was taken behind the Fullerton Hotel on

100. Rotherham Mandoline Band. The lady in the pale blouse on the left is Susan Beatrice Greaves, born 1889. She lived at the Red House, Mary Street, and married Gordon Eyre in 1918. The others remain a mystery, as does the time and place of the photograph, although it seems likely to have been in the early 1900s.

101-102. An open air performance of Shakespeare's *A Midsummer Night's Dream* at Roche Abbey on 15 and 16 July 1896, in aid of the Rotherham Hospital. Reserved seats were 5s (25p), unreserved half that and the enclosure 1s (5p) — substantial sums in those days. Oberon was played by Miss B Baines, Titania by Miss D Beam and Puck by Miss Nina Faydon, while Vivian D Stenhouse appeared as Bottom. At least four Beams took part.

103. The hoardings outsi[de] Sammy Moreton's boxi[ng] stadium in Effingham Street[,] the early part of 1937, probab[ly] February. Showing at the Reg[al] was the film of *My Man Godfr[ey],* starring William Powell a[nd] Carole Lombard, made in 193[6.]

104. The ring from across t[he] river on the same day. T[he] Grafton Hotel can be seen [at] the junction of Effingham Str[eet] and St Ann's Road. In its pla[ce] now stands The Comedi[an.] Sammy Moreton was a famil[iar] name in the town, for all sorts [of] reasons. He had fruit and fi[sh] shops in Effingham Stre[et,] Frederick Street and Wort[ley] Road, but also ran Sund[ay] afternoon wrestling shows [at] the Stadium. He died in 19[??] aged seventy-four.

. Heady days for Rotherham
unty, who won the Midland
ague every year between
1-12 and 1914-15 from their
llmoor base. They were
cted to the Second Division
he Football League in 1919,
relegated to the third in
3. Greater disaster was to
low: in the 1924-25 season
y won only seven games,
ishing bottom — eleven
nts behind next bottom
nmere. Amalgamation with
therham Town to form
ited came shortly after the
d of the season.

ROTHERHAM COUNTY F. C. 1911-12.

. Millmoor in 1930. The
voli Cinema and Henry
ay's department store can
seen at the top of the picture.

107-108. Views of College Square in the 1880s and 1890s, although at that time it was called Yard and not Square. The picture above cannot have been taken before 1881, because the premises on the left occupied by the Borough Boot Company were then used by Charles Tasker Fell, provision merchant. Equally, it cannot have been taken after 1889, because that was when an ornate lamp post appeared in the square. By 1890 the boot company, owned by Thomas Fieldhouse, had been replaced by Hydes and Company, milliners. Next door to Mr Fieldhouse was confectioner Charles Kenyon, of KP Nuts fame. The picture below was taken after 1890 and before 1898, when the Prudential Assurance Company moved from offices on the right of the picture to new premises in High Street. In 1891, or shortly afterwards, accountants Hart and Moss left College Chambers for Moorgate Street.